DRAW THE USA

AN EASY STEP-BY-STEP APPROACH

BY

Kristin J. Draeger

ART HISTORY CURRICULUM
DISGUISED AS FUN

Websites:
ArtK12.com
SeriousFunK12.com
info@artk12.com

Instructions

The Drawing

For this drawing use a plain 8 1/2 x 11 piece of paper turned horizontally. Follow the instructions in red, page by page, until the end of the book is reached, labeling the states as you go. It is helpful for the student, when drawing each step, to ask "Where does the line begin?" and "Where does it end?" It is also helpful to mark these beginnings and endings with a dot before drawing the line.

The map can be drawn all at once, but students may find it easier to master smaller portions of the map at a time. After drawing five or six states students may want to pause and practice what they have learned.

For younger students I recommend using ledger-sized (11x17) paper for drawing the maps. This size allows students with less refined motor skills to draw larger without worrying about running off the end of the page. This size of paper can be folded in half and stored in a 8 1/2 x 11 binder.

Coloring

If the student wishes to color the map, I recommend first inking it with a thin, black, permanent marker. This will help maintain the integrity of the outline and give the final product a more "professional" look.

Enjoy.

For Phineas with love,

edge of
paper

Leave a
little room
here . . .

Turn your paper sideways so that
it is wider than it is tall. In the
upper right corner draw a
rectangle that is slightly tilted
to the left.

Next draw a diagonal line that goes from near the top right corner to near the bottom left corner. Perfect. Now you have Vermont (VT) on the left and New Hampshire (NH) on the right.

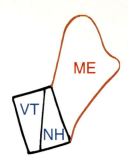

Next, draw a mitten-looking shape on the right side of the rectangle. Don't make the thumb part too pronounced; it's more of a thumb "bud." This is Maine (ME).

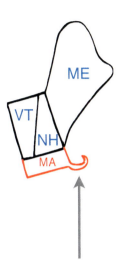

The hook-like thingy is Cape Cod.

Under the rectangle draw a short rectangle with a hook-like thingy. This is Massachusetts (MA).

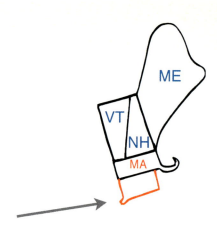

squarish
protrusion

Now draw another rectangle under
Massachusetts. This rectangle has
a squarish protrusion on the
bottom left side.

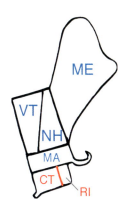

Divide the rectangle into two unequal parts. The left side is Connecticut (CT) and is larger. The right side is Rhode Island (RI) and is smaller.

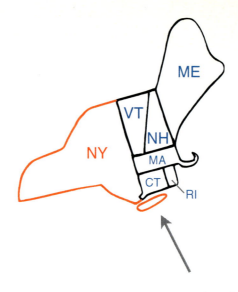

Long Island

New York (NY) begins at the top of Vermont and ends at the squarish protrusion on Connecticut. It also has a long island called . . . Long Island.

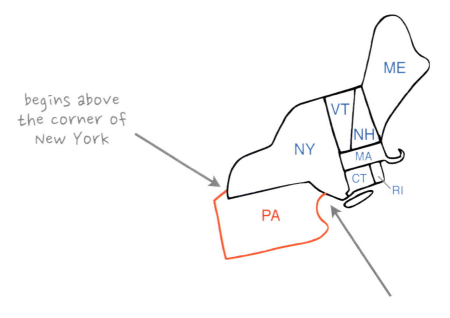

begins above
the corner of
New York

ends before
the bottom
of New York

Next is the state of Pennsylvania
(PA). Notice where its outline
begins and where it ends.

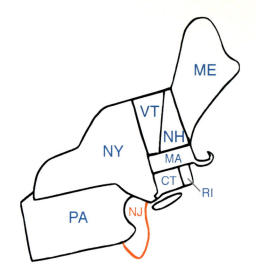

The eastern edge of New Jersey (NJ) is, appropriately, shaped like a "J." It begins near the bottom edge of New York and hooks up under Pennsylvania.

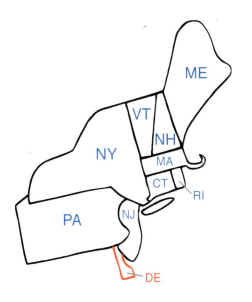

Delaware (DE) looks like a tiny square boot. Notice that the outline begins at Pennsylvania and ends at New Jersey.

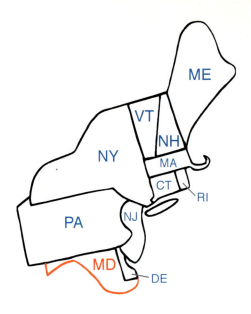

Maryland (MD) begins almost at
the corner of Pennsylvania and
ends at the tip of Delaware.

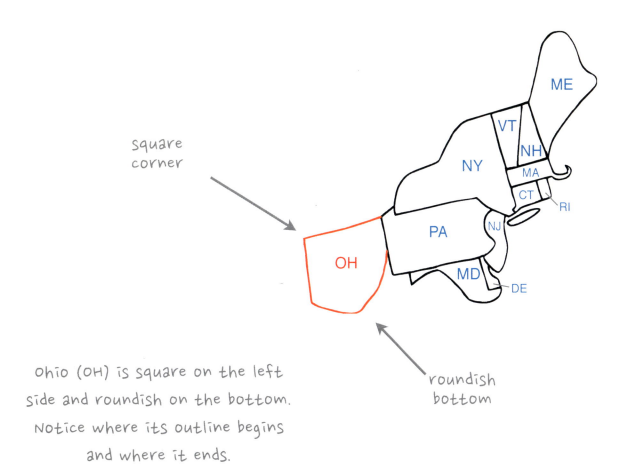

square corner

roundish bottom

Ohio (OH) is square on the left side and roundish on the bottom. Notice where its outline begins and where it ends.

INDIANA

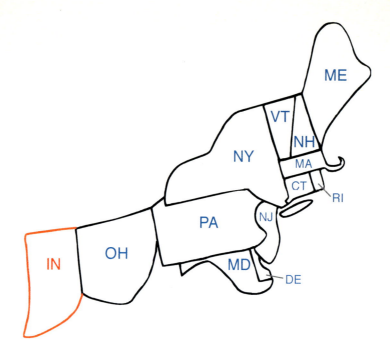

To the west of Ohio is Indiana (IN).
Notice that the outline begins and
ends at two of Ohio's corners.

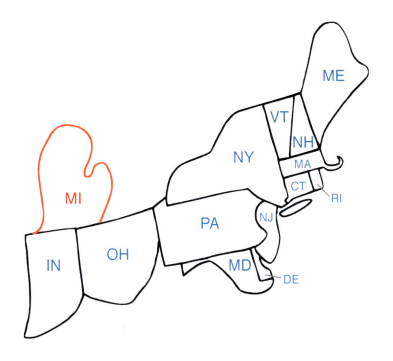

Michigan (MI) is another mitten, though this mitten has a more pronounced thumb than Maine's. It borders both Indiana and Ohio. Make sure it is a left-handed mitten.

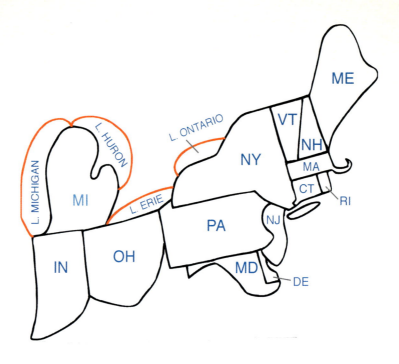

Next draw the Great Lakes. There are five lakes in all, but we will draw the fifth one later. Notice where the outlines touch each state.

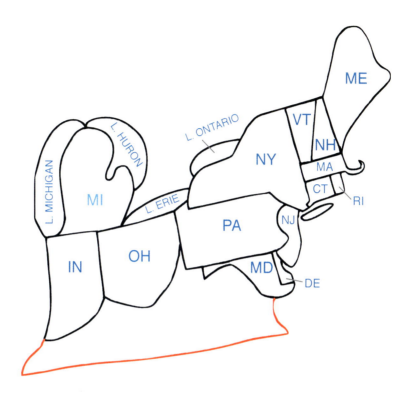

This is a blob that will be West Virginia, Kentucky and Virginia. The Appalachian Mountains run through these states so I call it the Appalachian Blob #1 (there will be more Appalachian Blobs later).

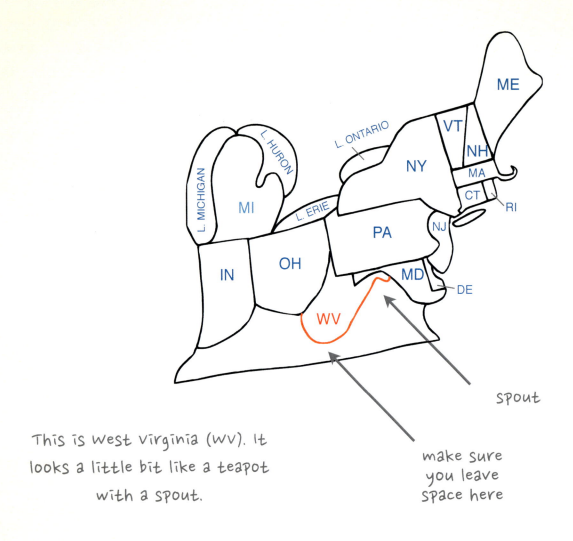

spout

This is West Virginia (WV). It
looks a little bit like a teapot
with a spout.

make sure
you leave
space here

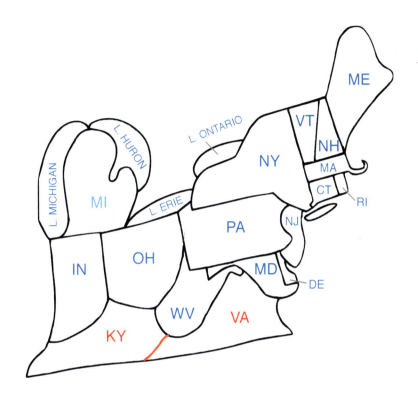

Splitting the last part of the blob into Kentucky (KY) and Virginia (VA) couldn't be easier.

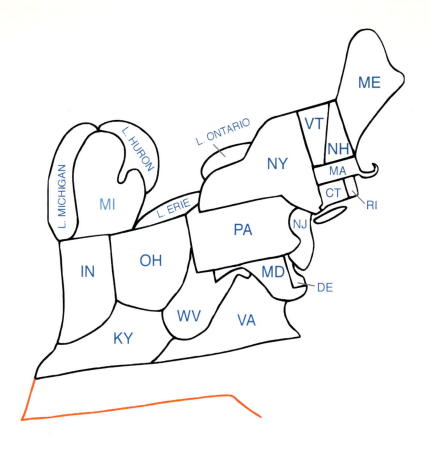

The Appalachian Mountains continue south through these next states so I call this blob the Appalachian Blob #2.

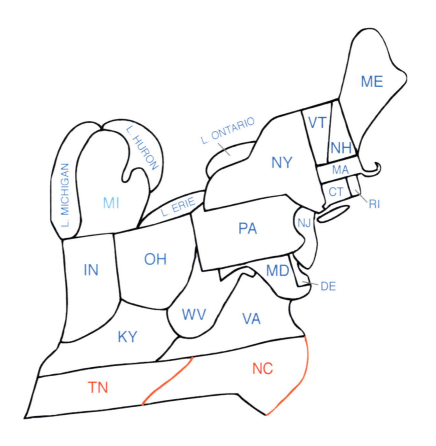

Separating the blob into
Tennessee (TN) and North
Carolina (NC) is easy.

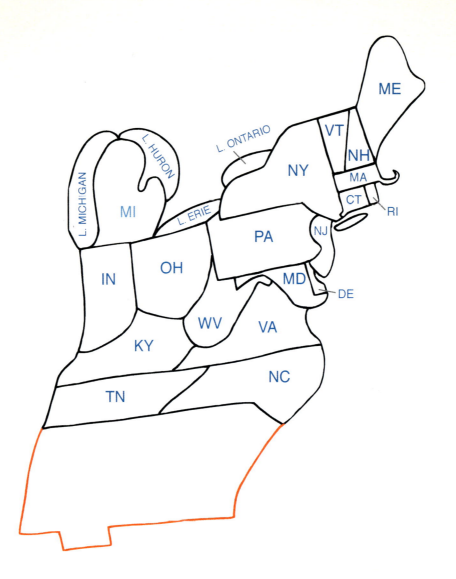

The Appalachians end in this third
and final blob.

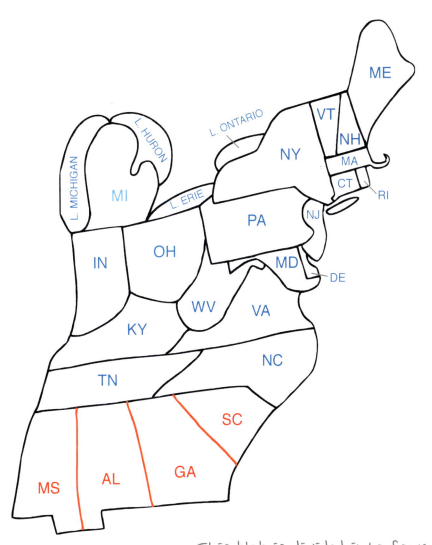

This blob is divided into four states: Mississippi (MS), Alabama (AL), Georgia (GA), and South Carolina (SC).

FLORIDA

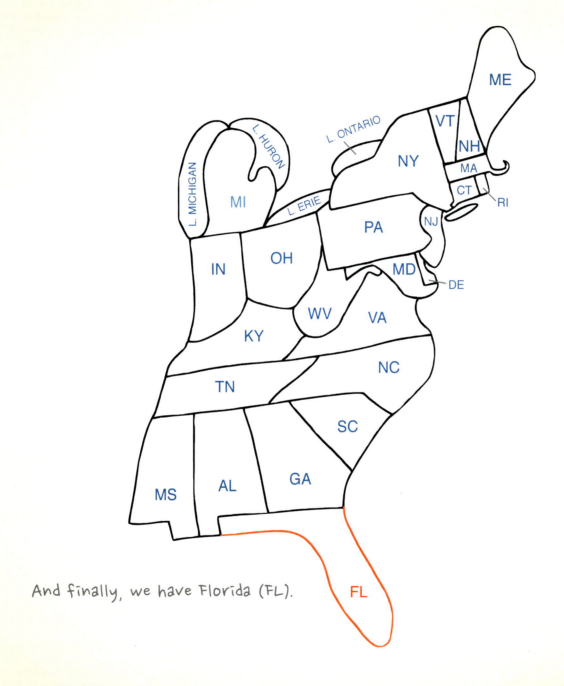

And finally, we have Florida (FL).

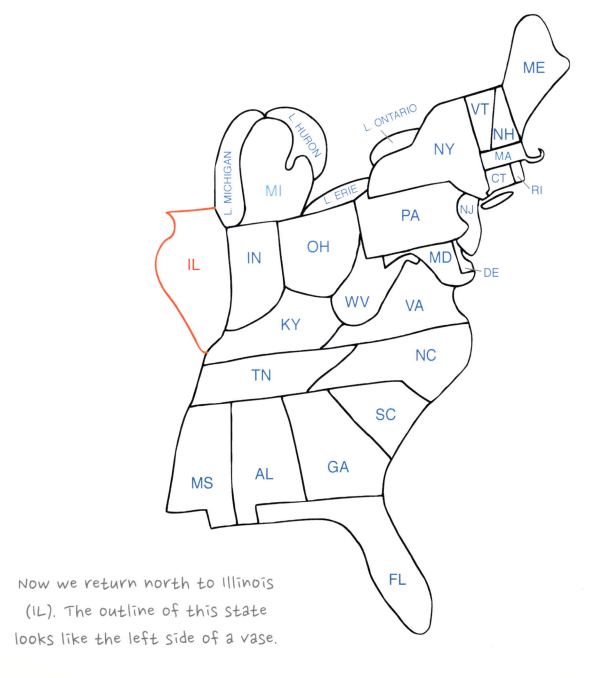

Now we return north to Illinois
(IL). The outline of this state
looks like the left side of a vase.

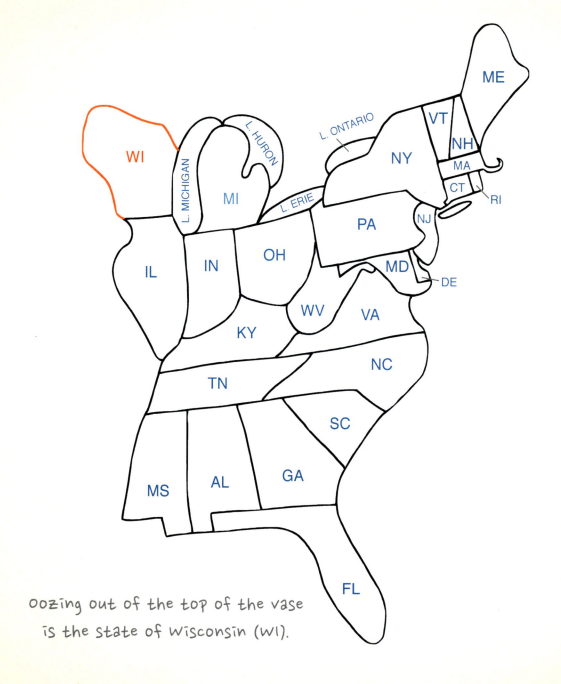

Oozing out of the top of the vase
is the state of Wisconsin (WI).

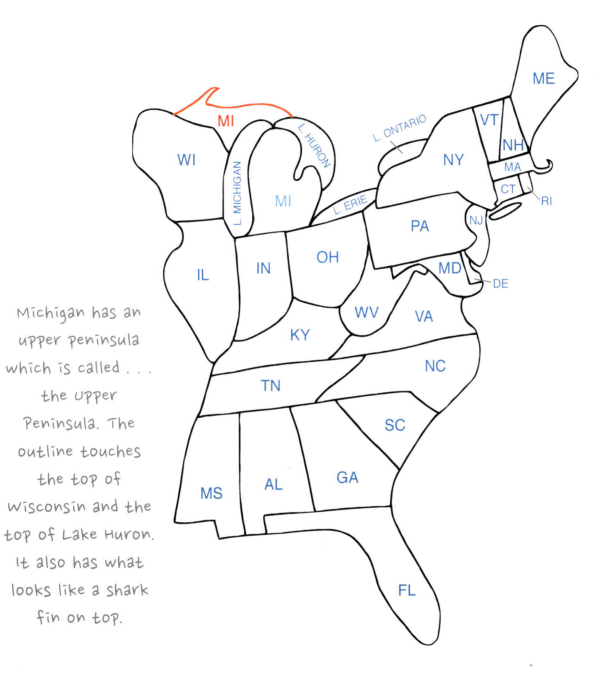

Michigan has an upper peninsula which is called . . . the Upper Peninsula. The outline touches the top of Wisconsin and the top of Lake Huron. It also has what looks like a shark fin on top.

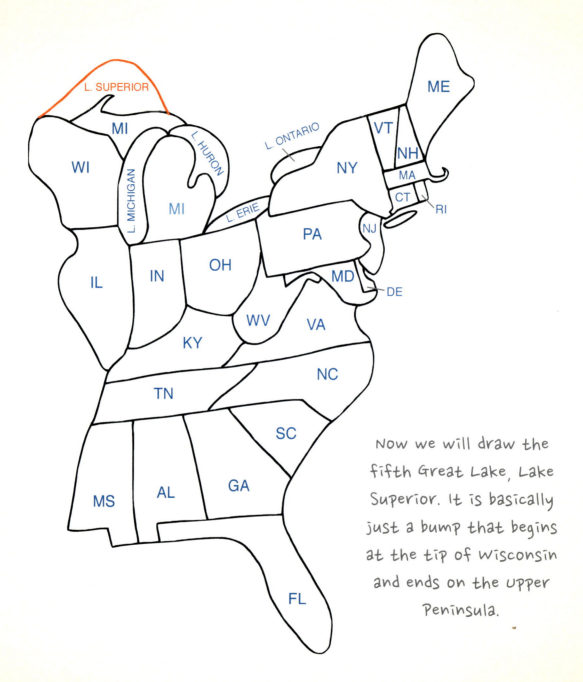

Now we will draw the fifth Great Lake, Lake Superior. It is basically just a bump that begins at the tip of Wisconsin and ends on the Upper Peninsula.

MINNESOTA

squarish
protrusion

triangular
protrusion

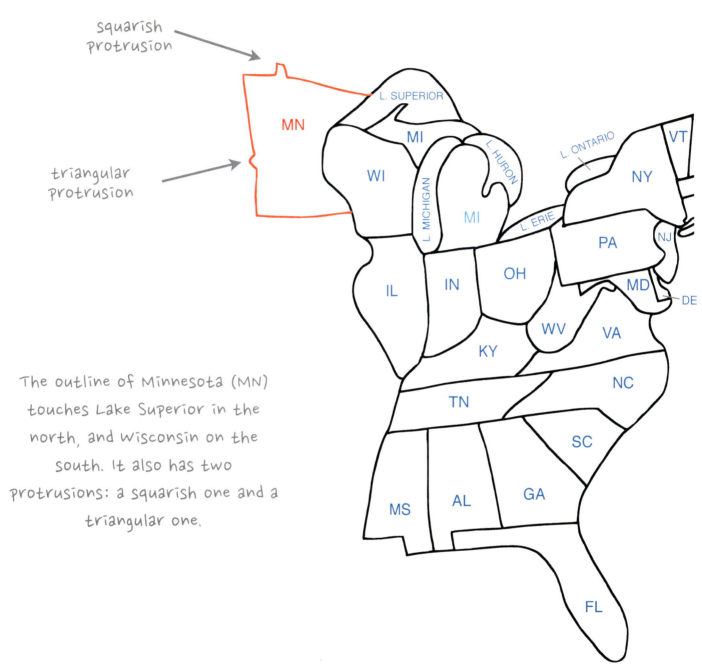

The outline of Minnesota (MN) touches Lake Superior in the north, and Wisconsin on the south. It also has two protrusions: a squarish one and a triangular one.

IOWA

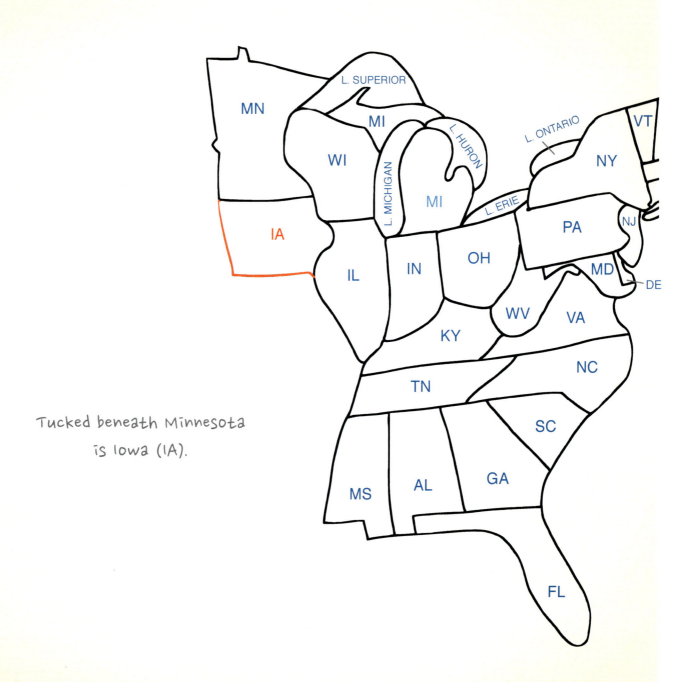

Tucked beneath Minnesota
is Iowa (IA).

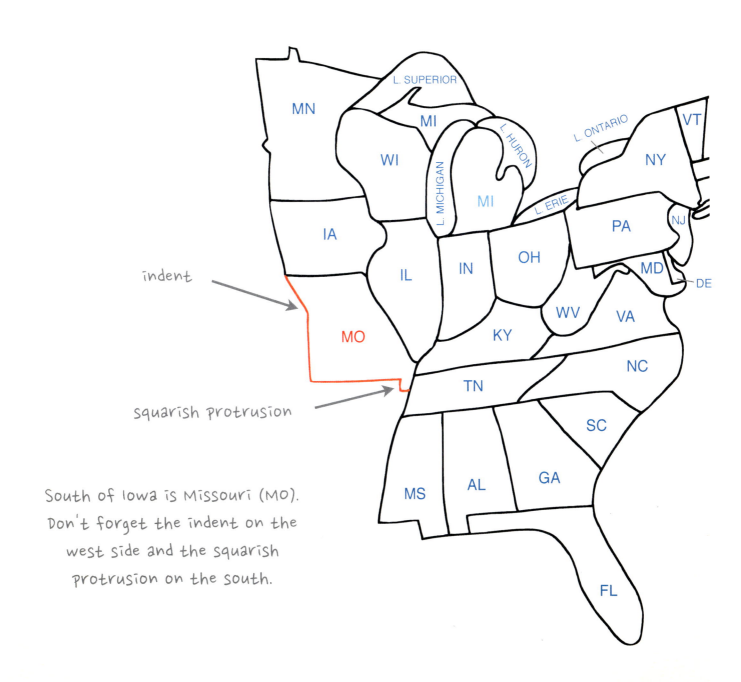

indent

squarish protrusion

South of Iowa is Missouri (MO).
Don't forget the indent on the
west side and the squarish
protrusion on the south.

ARKANSAS

square "bite"

South of Missouri is Arkansas (Ak).
It is a simple right angle with a
little square "bite" out of the
corner.

LOUISIANA

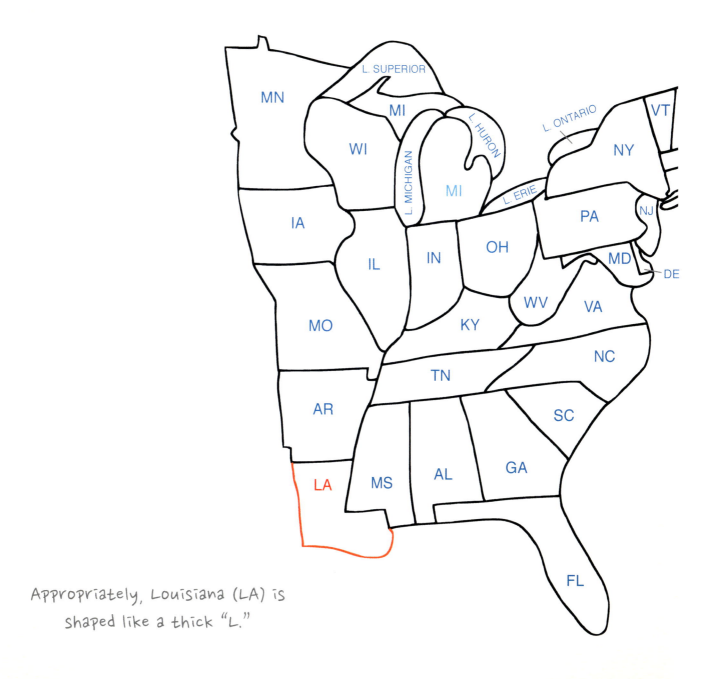

Appropriately, Louisiana (LA) is
shaped like a thick "L."

NORTH DAKOTA

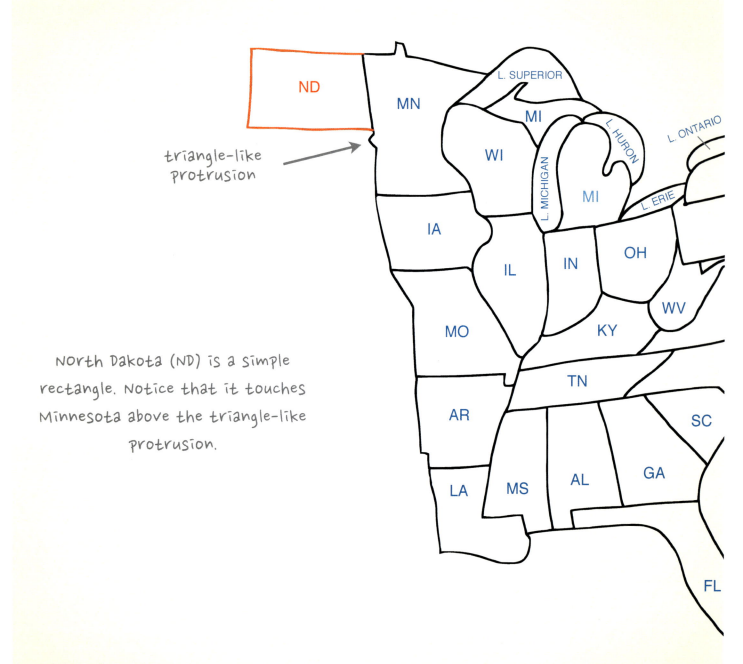

ND

triangle-like protrusion

North Dakota (ND) is a simple rectangle. Notice that it touches Minnesota above the triangle-like protrusion.

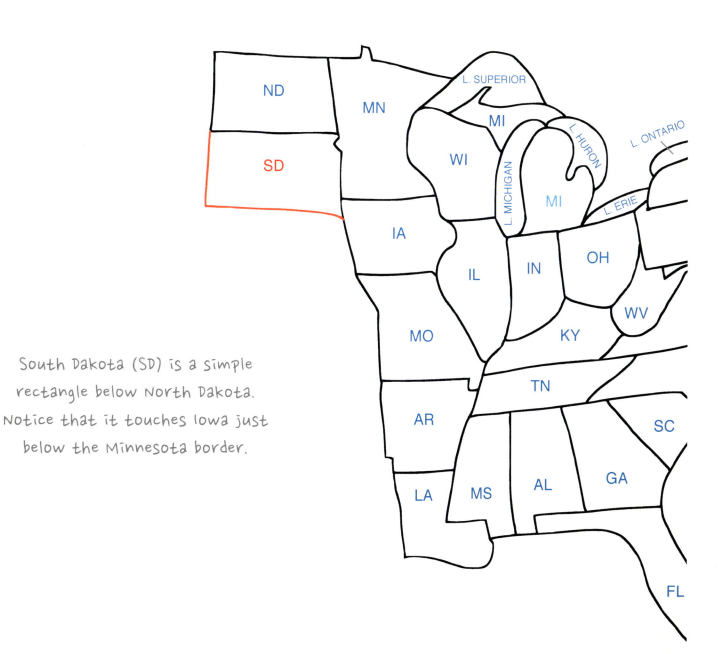

South Dakota (SD) is a simple rectangle below North Dakota. Notice that it touches Iowa just below the Minnesota border.

NEBRASKA

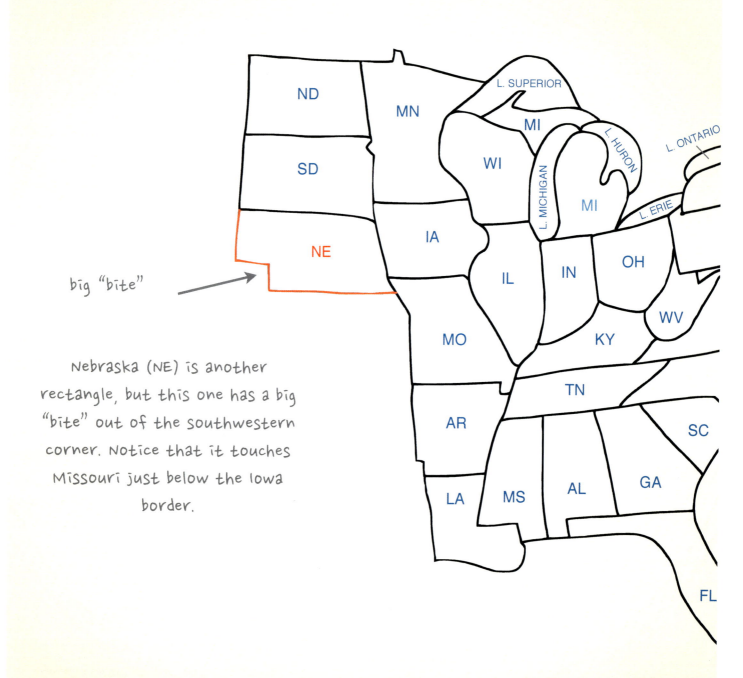

big "bite"

Nebraska (NE) is another rectangle, but this one has a big "bite" out of the southwestern corner. Notice that it touches Missouri just below the Iowa border.

KANSAS

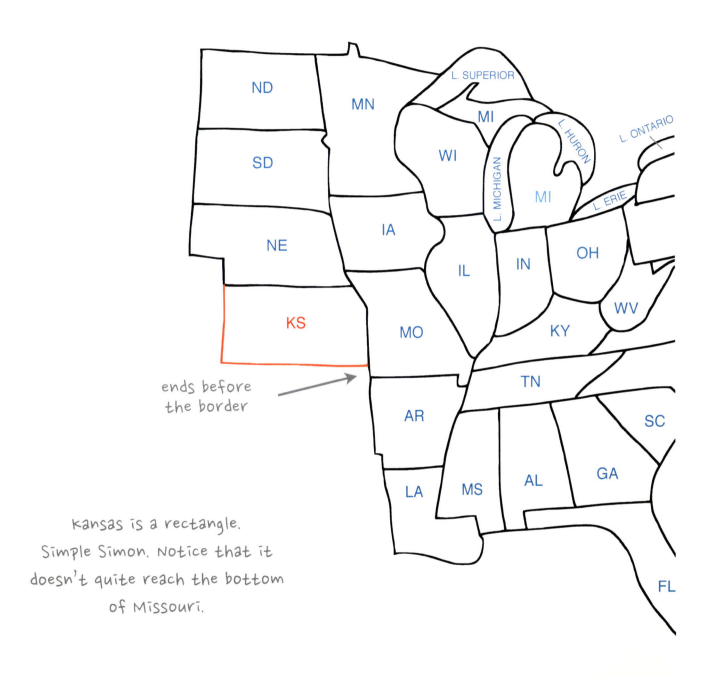

ends before
the border

Kansas is a rectangle.
Simple Simon. Notice that it
doesn't quite reach the bottom
of Missouri.

Panhandle

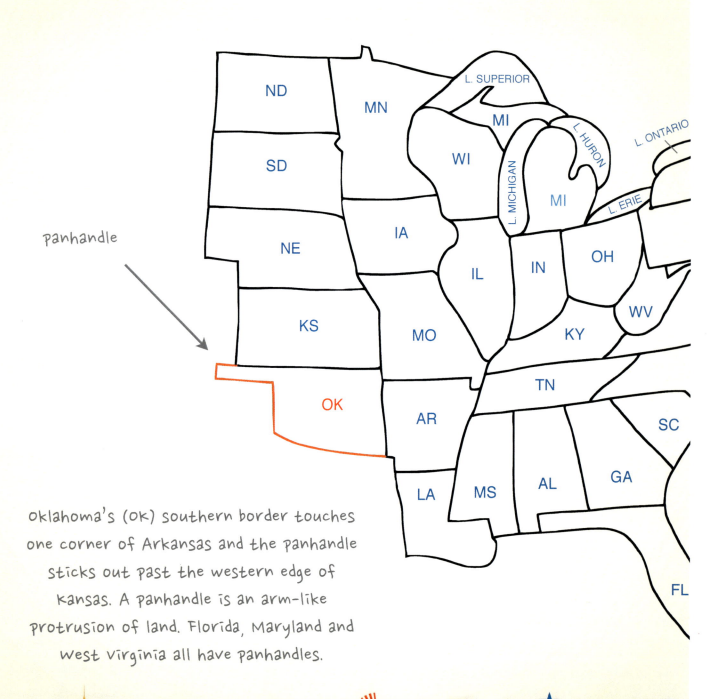

Oklahoma's (OK) southern border touches one corner of Arkansas and the panhandle sticks out past the western edge of Kansas. A panhandle is an arm-like protrusion of land. Florida, Maryland and West Virginia all have panhandles.

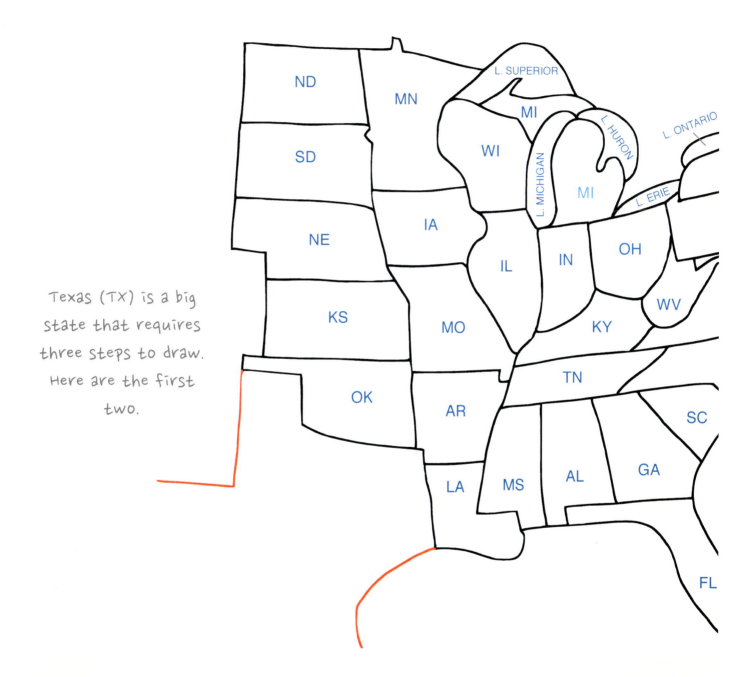

Texas (TX) is a big state that requires three steps to draw. Here are the first two.

TEXAS

Step three.

WYOMING

no touching
North Dakota

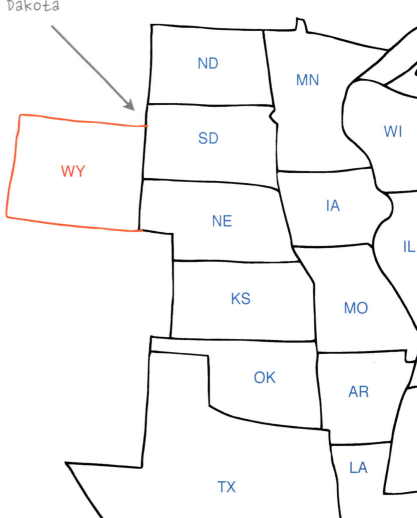

Wyoming (WY) is easy-peasy.
Notice that its northern border
is below the southern border of
North Dakota.

MONTANA

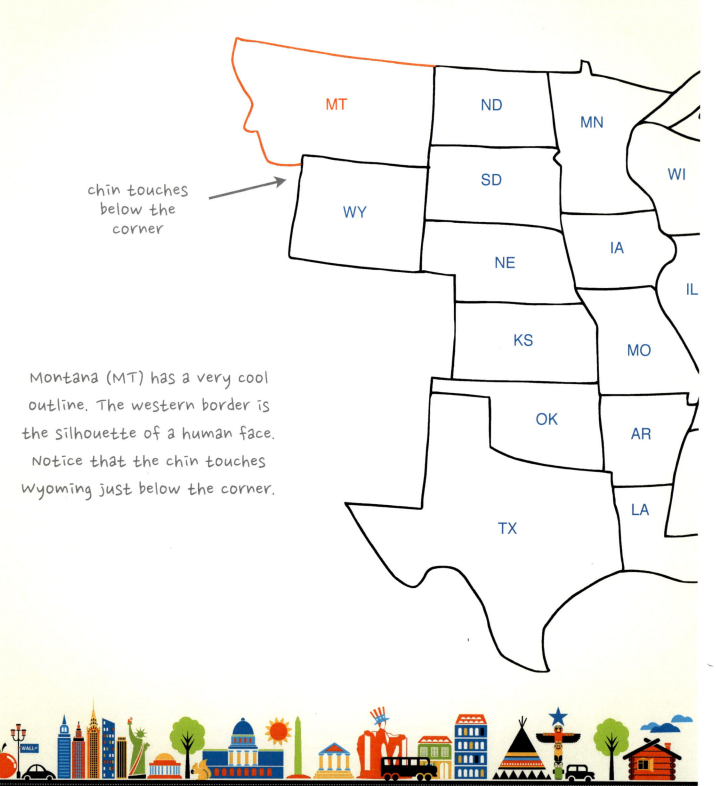

chin touches
below the
corner

Montana (MT) has a very cool
outline. The western border is
the silhouette of a human face.
Notice that the chin touches
Wyoming just below the corner.

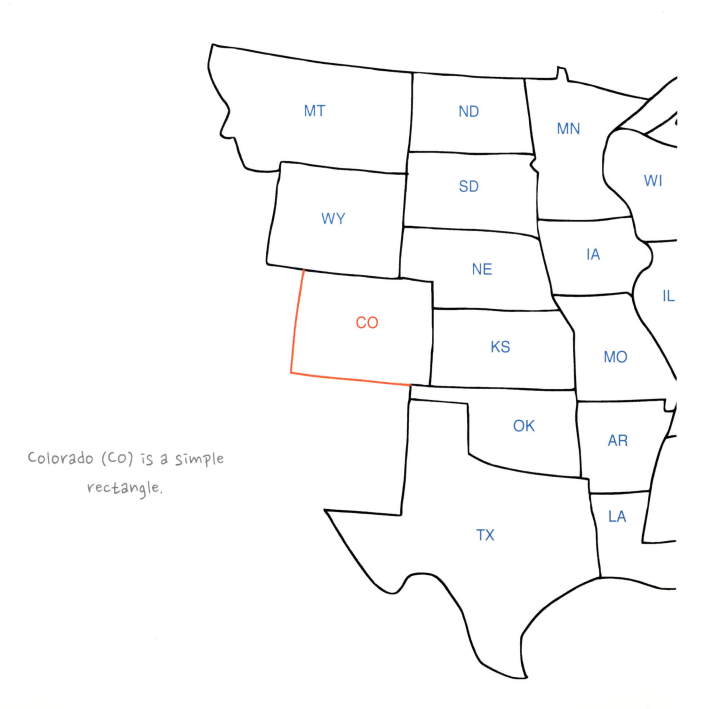

Colorado (CO) is a simple rectangle.

NEW MEXICO

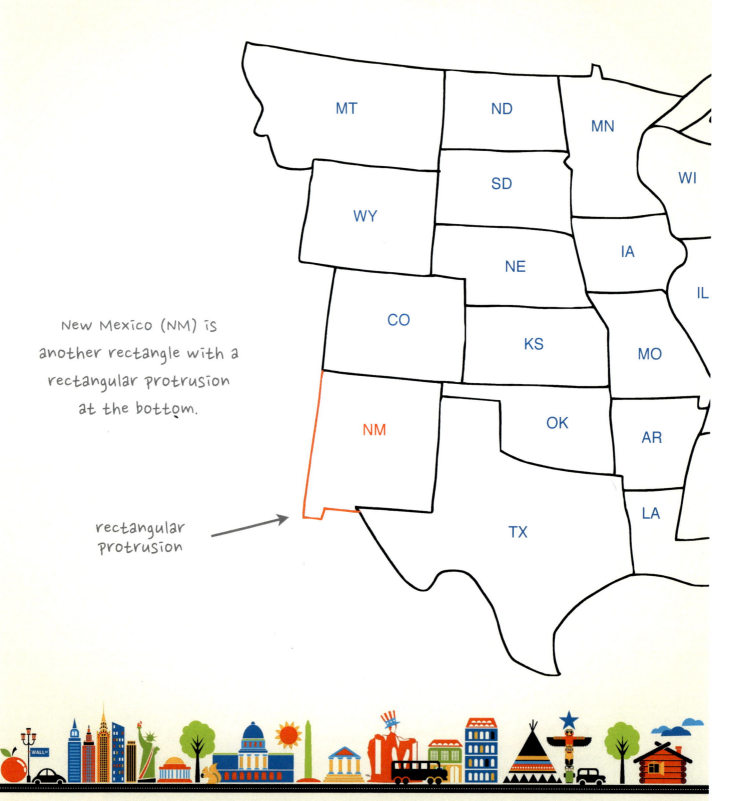

New Mexico (NM) is another rectangle with a rectangular protrusion at the bottom.

rectangular protrusion

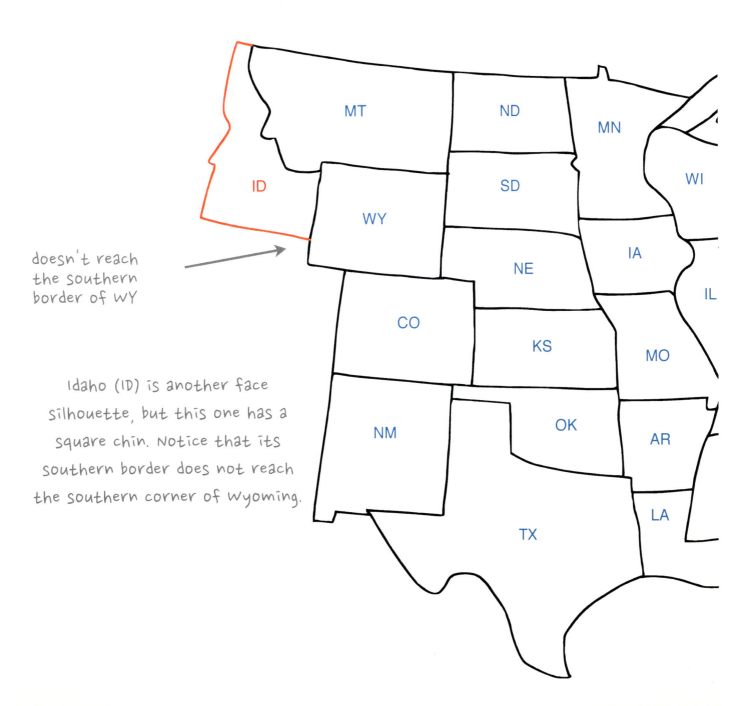

doesn't reach
the southern
border of WY

Idaho (ID) is another face
silhouette, but this one has a
square chin. Notice that its
southern border does not reach
the southern corner of Wyoming.

UTAH

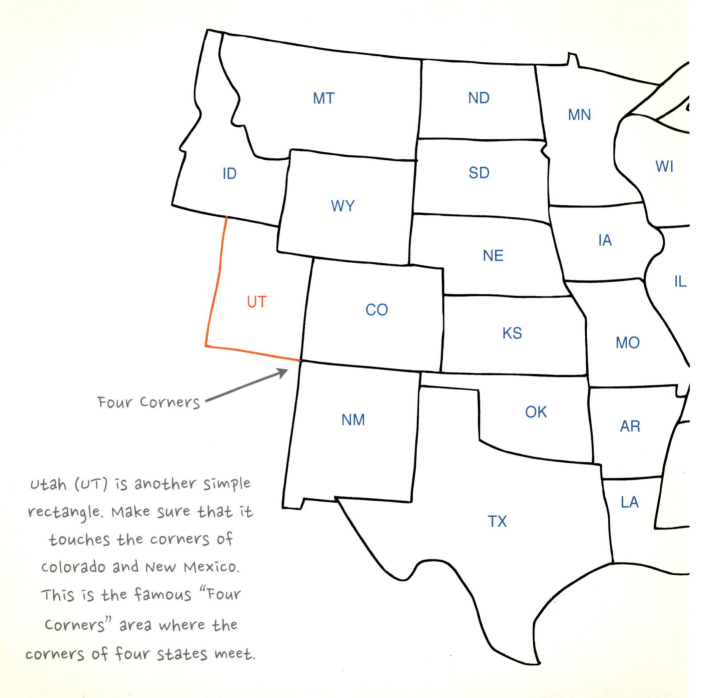

Four Corners

Utah (UT) is another simple rectangle. Make sure that it touches the corners of Colorado and New Mexico. This is the famous "Four Corners" area where the corners of four states meet.

ARIZONA

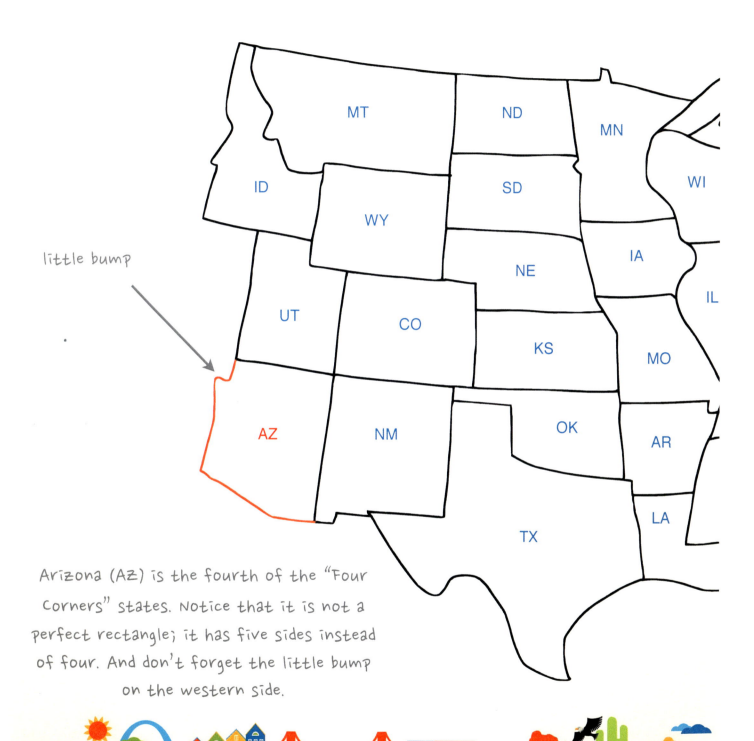

little bump

Arizona (AZ) is the fourth of the "Four Corners" states. Notice that it is not a perfect rectangle; it has five sides instead of four. And don't forget the little bump on the western side.

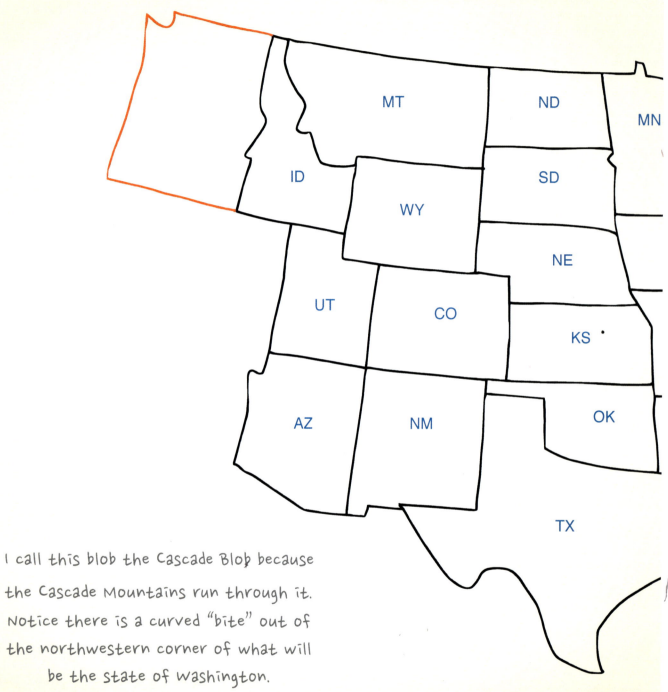

I call this blob the Cascade Blob because the Cascade Mountains run through it. Notice there is a curved "bite" out of the northwestern corner of what will be the state of Washington.

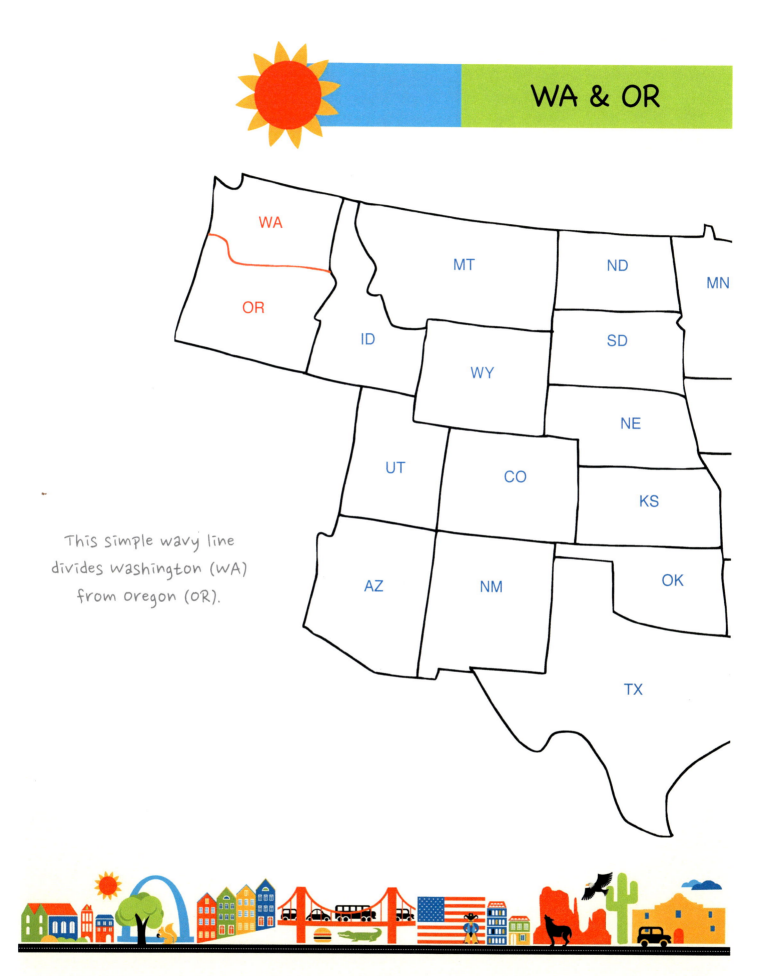

This simple wavy line divides Washington (WA) from Oregon (OR).

NEVADA

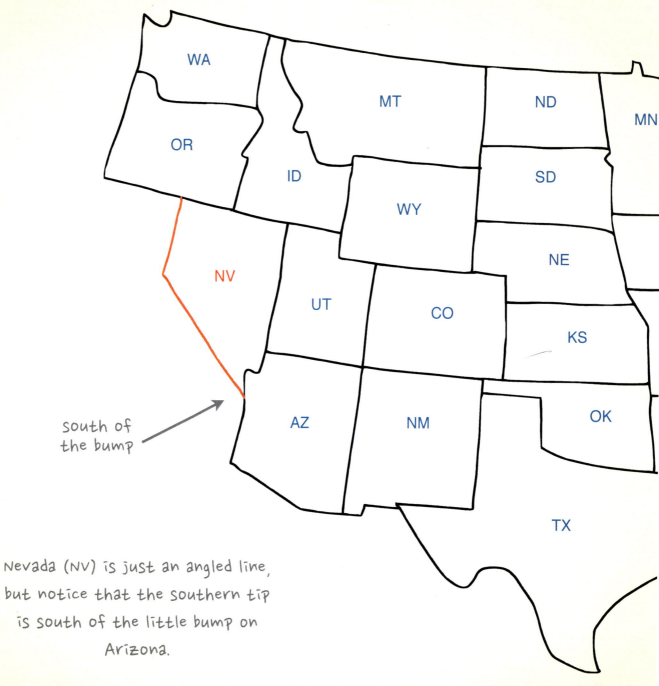

south of
the bump

Nevada (NV) is just an angled line,
but notice that the southern tip
is south of the little bump on
Arizona.

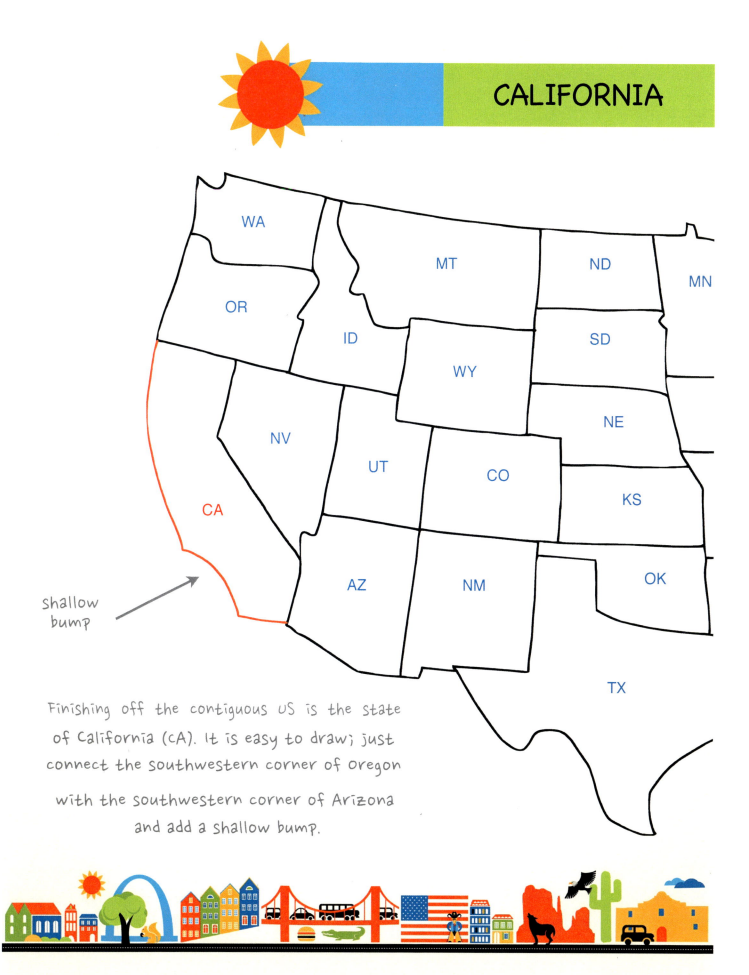

shallow bump

Finishing off the contiguous US is the state of California (CA). It is easy to draw; just connect the southwestern corner of Oregon with the southwestern corner of Arizona and add a shallow bump.

Alaska (Ak) is the largest and most complex state, so it will take a few steps to draw. Begin with a line at a slight angle.

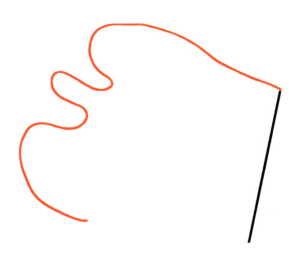

Then add three bumps. The middle bump should be skinnier than the other two.

Now add a two-armed octopus emerging out of the bottom of the state.

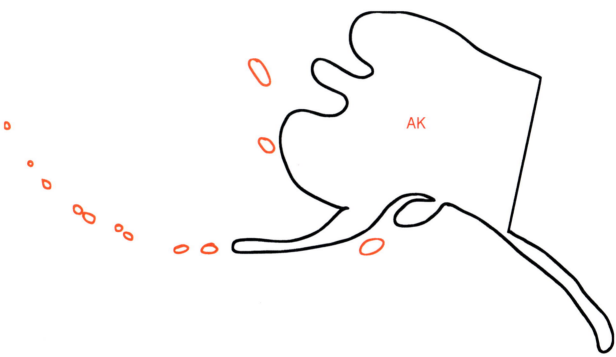

AK

Finally, add the islands. Alaska has 2,670 islands. You do not have to draw all of them, just a few of the larger ones will do.

ALASKA

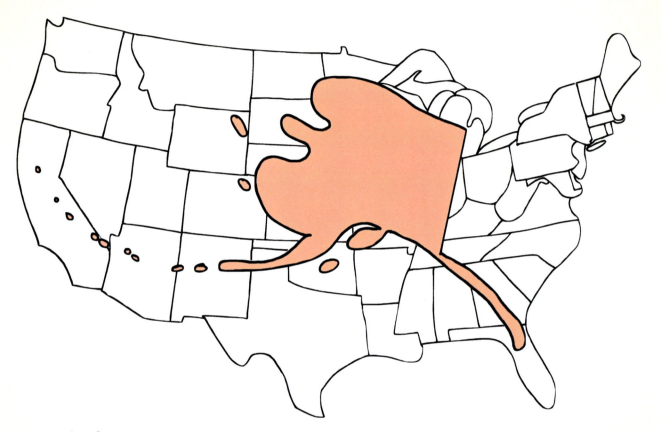

Alaska is by far the largest state in the Union, over twice the size of Texas.

HAWAII

Hawaii is comprised of eight main islands and over 100 other smaller islands.

HAWAII

Compared to the rest of the states, Hawaii is on the smallish side.

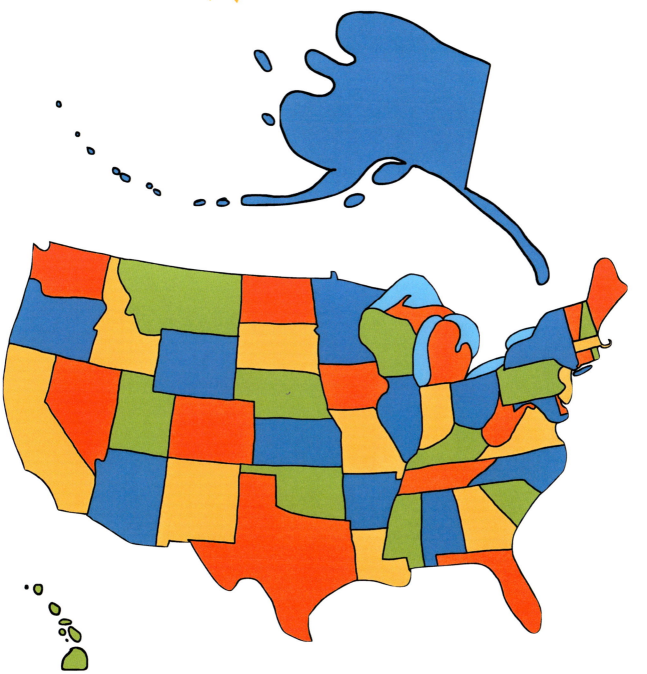

Congratulations! You have finished

drawing the USA! Yay!

Made in the USA
Columbia, SC
28 June 2019